The Mourner's Book of

Courage

30 Days of Encouragement

ALSO BY ALAN WOLFELT

The Mourner's Book of Hope: 30 Days of Inspiration

*Healing A Friend's Grieving Heart: 100 Practical Ideas
for Helping Someone You Love Through Loss*

Healing Your Grieving Heart: 100 Practical Ideas

The Journey Through Grief: Reflections on Healing

*Living in the Shadow of the Ghosts of Grief:
Step Into the Light*

*Understanding Your Grief: Ten Essential Touchstones
for Finding Hope and Healing Your Heart*

Companion Press is dedicated to the education and support of both the bereaved and bereavement caregivers. We believe that those who companion the bereaved by walking with them as they journey in grief have a wondrous opportunity: to help others embrace and grow through grief—and to lead fuller, more deeply-lived lives themselves because of this important ministry.

For a complete catalog and ordering information, write or call:

Companion Press
The Center for Life and Loss Transition
3735 Broken Bow Road
Fort Collins, Colorado 80526
(970) 226-6050

www.centerforloss.com

The Mourner's Book of

Courage

30 Days of Encouragement

ALAN D. WOLFELT, PH.D.

Companion
PRESS

An imprint of the Center for Loss and Life Transition

Fort Collins, Colorado

Companion Press is an imprint of the Center for Loss and Life Transition, 3735 Broken Bow Road, Fort Collins, Colorado 80526. www.centerforloss.com

Artwork by Christoph Kadur, www.istockphoto.com
Cover design and book layout by Angela P. Hollingsworth

Printed in Canada.

17 16 15 14 13 12   5 4 3 2 1

ISBN: 978-1-61722-154-5

Introduction

If you are reading this book, someone you love has died. There is no greater pain in life than the pain we feel when we are separated from someone we love. You might be unable to imagine how you can make it through the day, let alone move into the future. Your will and your spirit have been wounded. You are in the deep, inhospitable wilderness of grief. The only way out is to enter, to feel your grief with your whole, raw, open heart and soul. If you do this, and stay true to your unique journey through grief, you will be transformed—experiencing a "change in form"—and come out of the dark and into the light. Along the way you will need courage—courage to face your feelings, trust your instincts, travel your own path, and discover renewed meaning in your life and in your living.

What is Courage in Grief?

Courage stems from the Old French word for heart—*coeur*. Courage can be a small action or a large undertaking. Grief demands courage at almost every turn. It takes fortitude to rise and face the day when you know it will be filled with the pain of missing the person who died. It takes tenacity to take on a challenge alone, without that special person's assistance or insight. It requires backbone and integrity to let tears fall without immediately wiping them away. It takes boldness to accept a caring friend's shoulder or a relative's offer for help. Finally, it requires audacity to let grief and mourning come without trying to deny them or numb yourself with distractions. My hope is that these ideas on courageous grieving will buoy you up, each and every day, and help you authentically mourn in ways that relight your divine spark—that which gives your life meaning and purpose.

About This Book

This book is one in a series of three books for mourners. I wrote *The Mourner's Book of Hope* first, with the intent to help relight the divine spark in those who are deep in grief and mourning. Its purpose is to help people hold on to hope in dark moments and help them come to believe they will survive their grief. The purpose of this book is to not only companion people in grief and mourning while they walk their difficult journey, but to infuse them with courage and the will to continue on—to not only survive, but eventually thrive.

While this book is written in a linear fashion, please remember that your grief is not linear. It is very courageous to befriend your grief, to let it direct you rather than you trying to direct it. If you read a day's entry and you can't relate, turn to another one that better fits where you are in your grief journey. The book follows a 30-day format, but the acute phase of grief and mourning will take much longer, depending on the circumstances of the death and your relationship with the person who died. Grief can't be put on a schedule. My intent of making this a daily guide was simply to reflect that grief is a journey, and that it does change from beginning to end.

I wish you courage, grace, and comfort as you journey through your grief. Please view this little book as an encouraging friend who takes your hand and walks with you, by your side. As good friends do, let it fill you with strength and a belief that you can not only face your grief, you can be transformed by it.

My Prayer for You

May you discover courage in places both obvious and hidden along the way. May you face the emotions of your grief, which may include feelings of guilt, anger, sadness, fear, and loneliness. May you stay present to your grief and not turn away, but be filled with a commitment to see what it has to say. May you hold hope high like a candle in the dark and bravely walk forward, even when everything inside you urges you to turn and run.

May you find the fortitude to reach out when you are in trouble—at times when the pain is greatest and you need help from someone who cares about you and loves you, to regain the strength, hope, and courage it takes to continue on. May you, and you alone, decide what grief is like, and accept it for what it is, having the fortitude to look misconceptions in the face and set your own course—myths like, "Stay busy," "Let go," and "Get over it." It takes stoutheartedness to say no and set your own compass. It also takes bravery to know when you need to stop and rest, allowing yourself to embrace your grief in small doses rather than trying to tackle it all at once.

May you dedicate yourself to authentically mourn. May you release your grief through action—crying, sobbing, screaming, laughing, sharing rituals, talking with others, etc. Doing so honors the person who has died, acknowledges that love goes on, and manifests her spirit through action.

Finally, may you, over time and when you are ready, come to reconcile your grief. May you allow it to be a part of you but not let it control, or own, you. May you feel lightness and a sense of new freedom. May you embrace a new way of being and move with purpose. My final prayer for you is, through courage and determination, that you regain your footing and a belief that life is not only worth living, but worth celebrating and filling with meaning. With this new quiet strength, I pray that you march into the future—stronger and wiser, softer and sturdier—than ever before. Journey on, and choose life!

Alan D. Wolfelt

Day 1

Open to Loss

Whatever you do, you need courage.

~ Ralph Waldo Emerson

Believers, look up—take courage.
The angels are nearer than you think.

~ Billy Graham

Loss brings uninvited pain into our lives. In opening to the presence of the pain of your loss, in acknowledging the inevitability of the pain, in being willing to gently embrace the pain, you demonstrate the courage to honor the pain.

Honoring means "recognizing the value of" and "respecting." It is not instinctive to see grief and the need to openly mourn as something to honor, yet the capacity to love requires the necessity to mourn. To honor your grief is not self-destructive or harmful, it is courageous and life-giving.

The word express literally means "to press or squeeze out, to make known and reveal." Self-expression can change you and the way you perceive and experience your world. Transforming your thoughts and feelings into words gives them meaning and shape. Your willingness to honestly affirm your need to mourn will help you survive this difficult time in your life. Your spiritual purpose is not to repress or overindulge your emotions but rather to allow them so fully that they move through you.

The pain of grief will keep trying to get your attention until you unleash your courage and gently, and in small doses, open to its presence. The alternative—denying or suppressing your pain—is in fact more painful. If you do not honor your grief by acknowledging it, it will accumulate and fester. So, you must ask yourself, "How will I host this loss? What do I intend to do with this pain? Will I befriend it, or will I make it my enemy?"

You gain strength, courage, and confidence by every experience in which you really stop to look fear in the face. You are able to say to yourself, 'I lived through this horror. I can take the next thing that comes along.'

~ Eleanor Roosevelt

I have learned that the pain that surrounds the closed heart of grief is the pain of living against yourself, the pain of denying how the loss changes you, the pain of feeling alone and isolated—unable to openly mourn, unable to love and be loved by those around you. Instead of dying while you are alive, you can choose to allow yourself to remain open to the pain, which, in large part, honors the love you feel for the person who has died. After all, love and grief are two sides of the same precious coin.

As an ancient Hebrew sage observed, "If you want life, you must expect suffering." Paradoxically, it is the very act of mustering the courage to move toward the pain that ultimately leads to healing.

Courage is the most important of all the virtues, because without courage you can't practice any other virtue consistently. You can practice any virtue erratically, but nothing consistently without courage.

~ Maya Angelou

Personal Reflection on Courage

In what ways have I been opening to the presence of my loss?
In what ways have I perhaps been shutting out or denying the
presence of my loss?

_____

_____

_____

_____

_____

_____

_____

_____

_____

_____

_____

_____

_____

Day 2

Feast on Hope

Courage is like love; it must have hope for nourishment.

~ Napoleon Bonaparte

Courage is a kind of salvation.

~ Plato

Finding hope in the face of death can seem impossible. If someone you love has died, you might feel as if it's simply not worth going on. Yet, somehow you do. Somehow you get up in the morning and go about your day despite the heavy pressure that sits on your heart and threatens to break it open.

The strange, often surreal, thing about life is that it never stops. Often, the demands of life don't let you step off the ride and take the long, needed break that you deserve. It seems unbelievable, really, that you must partake, interact, and engage in life after a profound loss or tragedy.

What keeps you going? What stops you from simply curling up and dying yourself? Hope. Hope in the form of your own inner, divine spark—your own light that might be dimmed by loss but refuses to be put out—your internal energy that gives meaning, purpose, and fight to your life.

Feast on that hope. Embrace the belief that there will be days ahead when you can get through without crying, when you can go through an hour without feeling debilitated by thoughts of losing your loved one. Savor the knowledge that someday again you'll be able to smile and really mean it, laugh and feel real joy.

Until then, take in hope from wherever it resides and let it feed your inner flame. Maybe it lives in a beloved child's smile, a

Two qualities are indispensable: first, an intellect that, even in the darkest hour, retains some glimmerings of the inner light which leads to truth; and second, the courage to follow this faint light wherever it may lead.

~ Karl Von Clausewitz

blooming flower, the warmth of the sun on your face. Absorb its force, its light. Do you hear it in the voice of your best friend or a support group member who offers words of encouragement and reminds you that you are not alone? Someone who lets you know that there is life outside your pain? Or maybe it is in allowing yourself to simply breathe in and out as you shift into neutral for a while.

Take in this hope, this strength. Feed on it. After all, it's nourishment for courage. And it is courage that will carry you from moment to moment, day to day; courage that will lift you out of constant pain, hurt, and sadness; courage that will fuel your healing and help you walk into the wilderness of grief and enter the deep pool of mourning that, once experienced, prepares you for a future where you will be able to, once again, live a purposeful, joyful, and bountiful life.

Every day begins with an act of courage
and hope: getting out of bed.

~ Mason Cooley

Personal Reflection on Courage

What small joys fuel me throughout the day? What brings my life meaning? What makes my life worth living?

_____

_____

_____

_____

_____

_____

_____

_____

_____

_____

_____

_____

_____

Day 3

Take Grief's Hand

It is only through labor and painful effort, by grim energy and resolute courage, that we move on to better things.

~ Theodore Roosevelt

Someone you have given love to and received love from has died. You are grieving. You are "bereaved," which literally means you have been "torn apart" and have "special needs." You are beginning, or are in the midst of, a journey that is painful, often lonely, and naturally frightening.

Among your most special needs right now is to have the courage to grieve and mourn in a culture that doesn't always invite you to feel safe to do so. That said, I have written this book to help you draw forth your courage—the courage that already exists within you—to accept grief and mourning as they come.

There is a difference between grieving and mourning. Grief is the constellation of internal thoughts and feelings we have when someone we love dies. Mourning is when you take the grief you have on the inside and express it outside yourself. In other words, mourning is grief in action.

I encourage you to take grief's hand and let it lead you through the darkness and toward the light. You may not see the light at first, but forge ahead with courage, and with the faith that the light of hope and happiness does exist. Feel your pain, sorrow, sadness, disbelief, agony, heartbreak, fear, anxiety, and loneliness as much as you can.

This may seem odd, as these emotions could well be the ones you most want to avoid. You might fall into the common thinking of our society that denying these feelings will make them go away.

To have courage for whatever comes in life—everything lies in that.

~ Saint Teresa of Avila

You might have the urge to "keep your chin up" and stay busy and wait to "get over" your grief. Yet, ironically, the only way to help these hard feelings pass is to wade right into them. To get in and get dirty. Grief isn't clean, tidy, or convenient. All major life changes start with chaos and messiness. Yet feeling it and expressing it is the only way to feel whole once again. Grief that's not reconciled or integrated can leave you feeling "stuck" or empty. Your ability to engage in life could be inhibited, and you might feel like you've shut down.

Instead, choose grief. And as you walk with your grief, actively mourn in ways that are unique to your personality. Cry when you need to, call a friend when you feel overwhelmed, join a grief support group, express yourself through writing, music, dance, or sports. By taking action, you will eventually integrate the death of your loved one into your life. In exchange, you will find the hope, courage, and desire to once again live a full and rewarding life.

While walking with grief, remember two important things: 1) Grief and mourning have no timeline. Your grief journey is unique and will take as little or as much time as needed, depending on the unique circumstances of your loss. 2) Taking breaks along the way is needed and necessary. I like to use the word "dosing" when referring to grieving and mourning. Grief is not something you can do all at once. Feeling too many feelings and thinking too many thoughts can make you feel overwhelmed and totally emptied out. Instead, take in "doses" of grief and mourn in bits and pieces. Retreat and welcome respite as needed.

Grief may never leave your side, but it will allow you to let go and venture forth on your own more and more as days, weeks, months, and years pass. Tap into your innate courage and accept the hand of those people who support, love, and nurture you.

Personal Reflection on Courage

What feelings of grief are coming up strongest for me today? What am I doing with these feelings? Am I befriending them or am I fighting against them?

_____

_____

_____

_____

_____

_____

_____

_____

Day 4

Befriend Courage

The strongest, most generous, and proudest of all virtues is true courage.

~ Michel de Montaigne

What is courage? When you think of courage, images of bravery might come to mind—knights on horseback charging the line, firefighters risking their lives to rescue a family from a burning building, or hikers summiting Mount Everest. This is bravery, not courage. Bravery is loud and boisterous. Courage is soft and quiet. Without the steady, quiet resolve and unfailing commitment of courage, bravery would never happen. Courage is what fuels bravery. It is the bridge between fear and action. It is a still, quiet voice encouraging you to go on.

Bravery is daring and doing; courage is friendly and welcoming. Find ways to make friends with courage. To "befriend" literally means making an effort to "become friends." Imagine what it would be like to have courage as a friend who walks beside you at all times: a friend who never nags, never pushes, but simply places a gentle hand on your back and whispers words of encouragement, helping you take the next step, and the next. With courage by your side, you are able to go on, to walk through your days and do the next right thing.

Cultivate a relationship with courage every day. Each morning, welcome courage. Before you rise, say your favorite quote on courage out loud. Maybe it is the Serenity Prayer, borrowed from Alcoholics Anonymous, and one of my favorites: "God, grant me the serenity to accept the things I cannot change,

And the day came when the risk it took to remain tight inside the bud was more painful than the risk it took to blossom.

~ Anais Nin

courage to change the things I can, and the wisdom to know the difference." Or maybe there's one that you especially like in this book. If you want, write down your favorite quotes on courage and put them on your fridge, dashboard, mirror, or computer at work. This will help you keep courage close, all day long.

Look for simple ways to give voice to courage throughout the day. Maybe it is simply having the ability and courage to get out of bed. But maybe it's the courage to share how you feel about your loss with a coworker or friend, or to walk through the doors of a grief support group. It could simply be making a phone call you've been putting off, writing a thank you to someone who helped after the funeral, going to a place of worship alone, or finding the capacity to be honest with yourself about something you fear. Healing after a death is hard. It takes courage in all shapes and sizes to mourn fully while living day to day. Congratulate yourself on welcoming courage, regardless of its size or reach.

Personal Reflection on Courage

In what ways can I befriend courage every day? If courage was a friend walking beside me, what words of encouragement would I want to hear? Who in your life seems to be able to empower you with courage?

_____

_____

_____

_____

_____

_____

_____

_____

_____

_____

_____

_____

Day 5

Voice Your Feelings

One isn't necessarily born with courage, but one is born with potential. Without courage, we cannot practice any other virtue with consistency. We can't be kind, true, merciful, generous, or honest.

~ Maya Angelou

It takes courage to grieve. I know a woman who lost her husband in a tragic car-bike accident. The timing for tragedy is never good, but for her, it was downright cruel. They had just gotten married, bought a house, and were looking forward to starting a family. Her shock and disbelief were overwhelming. She asked all the big questions. She felt every emotion: anger (over the driver's carelessness), guilt (for being short with him in their last conversation), terrible sadness (over losing him and their future), and countless others. But she allowed herself to express her many thoughts and feelings.

This woman fell into a habit of walking with a good friend a few times a week. While they walked, she talked. She'd mull over what happened, and how it could have been prevented; she'd nearly scream with rage about how the driver wasn't taking any responsibility, and how his carelessness took her husband's life. For a year straight, they kept up this ritual.

I admire her for her bravery to voice her feelings—to share them as many times as she needed to—day after day after day. She was not going crazy by talking about the death over and over again. She was simply "telling her story."

During this difficult time, you may feel okay one minute and in the depths of despair the next. As best you can, accept these sudden mood changes. You may also experience "griefbursts"—sudden feelings of overwhelming grief accompanied by anxiety

Life shrinks or expands in proportion to one's courage.

~ Anais Nin

and pain. Griefbursts can crash into you like an unexpected wave. You have no choice but to give in to the force of the crest, letting it toss you and twist you, leaving you unsteady and off-balance. This feeling of uncertainty is another common grief emotion. Accept it as best you can.

You may also feel an unending need to cry and sob. Sobbing comes from deep in your core. It is another way, besides talking, to express your deep emotions. Sobbing can feel like you have lost control, but by allowing yourself to sob you give voice to your authentic, deep grief. This is extremely important, because oftentimes grief is beyond words.

Grief is hard to feel and mourning is hard to let happen, but allowing your feelings to surface and honoring them with words and actions will help you integrate your loss. With active mourning comes the chance to let your grief move through you, leaving you changed, but intact. The alternative is burying your grief feelings deep inside where they settle and harden on your heart, making it difficult for you to feel, move, and grow. The result is that you risk dying while you are alive.

Personal Reflection on Courage

When you think of sharing your emotions with someone, who comes to mind? Can you call that person right now and arrange to meet, or at least talk on the phone? Can you request that she be on "standby" for times when you really need to talk? Better yet, can you ask her to commit to a regular visit? If talking is difficult for you right now, what other ways can you allow yourself to acknowledge what you think and feel?

_____

_____

_____

_____

_____

_____

_____

_____

_____

_____

Day 6

Reveal Your Protest Emotions

Hope has two beautiful daughters - their names are anger and courage; anger at the way things are, and courage to see that they do not remain the way they are.

~ St. Augustine

You may not be feeling anger, but if you are, it's important to see anger for what it is: a protest. Explosive, protest emotions like anger, hate, blame, terror, resentment, rage, and jealousy may be a volatile yet natural part of your grief journey. All these feelings are a reaction to feeling ripped off or treated unfairly. Imagine a toddler who has a toy yanked out of his hands. He wants the toy, so his instinctive reaction is to scream, cry, hit, or wail with anger. When someone loved is taken from you, your intuitive reaction might be similar. Our human instinct is to want back what we lost and valued.

You may be asking a lot of Why questions, like "Why me, why us?" or "Why did this have to happen?" You may want to find someone to blame—a doctor, the polluting power company, friends, family members, and maybe even the person who died.

You may want to hide your protest emotions from others. After all, these feelings can be scary for both the one feeling it and the one receiving it. Yet if you hold it inside, you will most likely feel bad physically (upset stomach, tension, poor sleep) or emotionally (irritability, feeling stuck). Be aware that you have two avenues for expression—outward or inward. The outward leads to healing, the inward does not. Pent-up anger can come out sideways as irritation at others—coworkers, the person driving in front of you, or the grocery store clerk.

Courage is not simply one of the virtues, but the form of every virtue at the testing point.

~ C.S. Lewis

If we're growing, we're always going to be out of our comfort zone.

~ John Maxwell

It helps to remember that protest emotions often mask other feelings—feelings of hurt, helplessness, frustration, and fear. When you feel anger rising up, ask yourself: What is driving this anger? Do I feel hurt? Vulnerable? Mistreated? Consider the positive effects of anger. Anger can serve as a catalyst for action, moving you forward.

Resolve to find a healthy way to express your anger. Share your feelings of anger with people you trust, letting them know that you need to express your feelings, and you don't need them to offer a solution, just an open, non-judging heart. Be clear and direct. Remind yourself that explosive emotions are not good or bad, or right or wrong. They just are. They are symptoms of a hurt that needs nurturing, not judging.

If you feel physically pent up, release anger in a creative way that fits your personality—join a kickboxing class at your gym, take up running and charge up hills, attack your garden with a sharp shovel or hoe, take a sledgehammer to a wall and open up a room, or get a drum set and pound away. Finally, practice relaxation to calm your racing heart and tense muscles. Listen to a relaxation CD or attend a yoga or meditation class.

If you deal with anger in a healthy way as it comes up, you'll lessen its intensity and duration as you mourn. Remember, you can't go around or over your grief. You must go through it—as uncomfortable as that seems. Helen Keller was right: "The only way to the other side is through."

Personal Reflection on Courage

Have you experienced anger or other protest emotions during your grief journey? If so, how have you dealt with it so far? Do you have a person you trust who allows you to explore these "survival-oriented" emotions? If so, who is that person? If not, who can you turn to for support and understanding?

_____

_____

_____

_____

_____

_____

_____

_____

_____

_____

_____

_____

Day 7

Uncover Your Guilt

Far better is it to dare mighty things, to win glorious triumphs, even though checkered by failure, than to take rank with those poor spirits who neither enjoy much nor suffer much because they live in the gray twilight tthat knows neither victory nor defeat.

~ Theodore Roosevelt

There's no problem so awful that you can't add some guilt to it and make it even worse.

~ Bill Watterson

As with anger, some people experience guilt after someone loved has died. Guilt, regret, shame, and self-blame are hard emotions to feel. Unchecked, they can lead to depression, a sense of hopelessness, and complicated grief.

It is natural to look back and think about what could have been done to create a different outcome. Maybe you are exploring your "if onlys." As in, "If only I had made her go to the doctor sooner." And, "If only I had said no, and told him to come straight home that day." In my mother's situation after my father's death from malignant melanoma, it was, "If only I had seen that mole on his back sooner."

"If onlys" are spinning tops. If you find yourself having "if only" thoughts, be gentle with yourself. Remind yourself that you are not to blame. It's impossible to go through life without saying or doing something you later wish you could change. Trust that you did the best with the information you had in the moment. We are not fortunetellers or all-powerful. We are human.

Explore whether you are feeling any of these common aspects of guilt and regret during grief:

- Survivor Guilt. Includes thoughts of "why him, not me?" with wishes that you had died instead.
- Relief Guilt. If the one you loved suffered before death, you may have felt relief when she died. This can bring on

I get up and pace the room, as if I can leave my guilt behind me. But it tracks me as I walk, an ugly shadow made by myself.

~ Rosamund Lupton

undeserved guilt. The same can happen when you don't miss certain aspects of your relationship or times when it was difficult.

- Joy Guilt. Feeling joy, or happiness might feel disrespectful to the person who died, or disloyal to your relationship. Of course, this isn't true. Imagine your loved one laughing or smiling along with you—celebrating the fact that you can experience moments of joy once again.

Be brave and find a friend or counselor with a compassionate ear to share any potential feelings of guilt and regret with. Your friend might find it strange that you are having such feelings. Remind her that however illogical your feelings and ideas sound, you need to explore their base, their reality. In the end, whether you erred in some way is beside the point. Remind yourself you made the best choice or gave the most appropriate response as you could at the time. No one is perfect, and there are some things in life you cannot change. As much as you can, allow yourself to do "if only" work of mourning with an understanding companion.

Open to self-forgiveness and self-love. Here's an exercise that helps: Close your eyes and picture your current self sitting next to your past self. Now, put a comforting arm around your old self's shoulder. Feel compassion flow from you for the pain she is feeling. Comfort her, like you would a good friend or child.

Personal Reflection on Courage

Do you have any regret or guilt feelings about things that happened in the past or while your loved one was dying? How can you release these feelings? Who do you trust to be a good listener? If you feel stuck or seem to be punishing yourself in any way, give yourself the gift of seeking help from a caregiver.

_____

_____

_____

_____

_____

_____

_____

_____

_____

_____

_____

_____

Day 8

Sit in Sadness

*Have courage for the great sorrows of life
and patience for the small ones; and when
you have laboriously accomplished your daily
task, go to sleep in peace. God is awake.*

~ Victor Hugo

Courage is found in unlikely places.

~ J.R.R. Tolkien

At times, it's courageous to do nothing. When you hurt deeply, it's tempting to fill every moment of the day so you don't have to feel your pain. It takes courage to turn down an invitation or resist being busy and instead stay home and sit and be still in sadness.

You might think, "being sad won't do me any good." Paradoxically, the only way to lessen your pain is to move toward it. As you experience your sadness, you are taking steps on a long journey toward integration of your loved one's death and a new, and hopefully, fulfilling future. This may seem impossible early on, but as you move through your grief, the light of it gets brighter with each step.

Sadness unexpressed can become or resemble depression, with symptoms such as sleep disturbances, appetite changes, decreased energy, withdrawal, lack of concentration, a sense of loss of control, and even thoughts of suicide. If these feelings make it hard to function at home and work, seek the help of a professional counselor.

Sadness will most likely accompany you on your entire journey, and stay with you to some degree for quite some time. Weeks or even months may pass before you even feel the full depth of your sorrow. Yet this is how it should be, as encountering your loss and sadness all at once would be impossible to tolerate.

Don't wish me happiness. I don't expect to be happy all the time.... It's gotten beyond that somehow. Wish me courage and strength and a sense of humor. I will need them all.

~ Anne Morrow Lindbergh

You may feel sadness so deeply that it threatens to break you in two. During these times, it's okay to dose yourself—to feel sadness, but then take a break and do something soothing. Staying aware of your own moment-to-moment needs and your own unique grief journey takes daring and courage, especially when you encounter others who are uncomfortable with your sadness. Disregard any well-meaning but misinformed advice to "move on," "be strong," and "don't be sad."

Of course you feel sad. Someone you cared for deeply has died. The landscape of your world has changed, and you feel unsure of how to navigate it. You may feel sadder during specific times—weekends, holidays, family meals, anniversaries, and waking up in the morning or arriving home to an empty house.

When you feel able, take a risk and invite sadness to sit down beside you. As sadness speaks, listen without interruption. Allow its words to wash over you. Respond with honesty—cry, wail, sob, yell, scream, or weep—to let sadness know that it's been heard.

Personal Reflection on Courage

Am I willing to sit with my sadness today? Have I been trying to stay busy so I don't feel sad? Who can I trust to help me enter into my sadness and not feel a need to take it away?

_____

_____

_____

_____

_____

_____

_____

_____

_____

_____

_____

_____

Day 9

Face the Giant

No one ever told me that grief felt so much like fear.

~ C.S. Lewis

Courage is being scared to death -
but saddling up anyway.

~ John Wayne

Fear undefined and unchallenged can feel like a threat to your well-being, not unlike what it would feel like to face a giant.

Likely, the death of the person you have given love to and received love from creates some fundamental fears, like "What does my future hold?", "Who am I, alone?", and, "How do I fill my days, my time?", and finally, "Will I be okay?" These questions are natural. Your sense of safety and security has been threatened, so you understandably feel anxious and afraid.

It takes courage to ask these questions, to tease them out from the tangled mass of fear that they have become. All balled up they can carry a punch. They can cause panic attacks, anxiety, and a sense of being frozen and unable to move. Some people I have companioned through grief describe this giant mass of fear as a feeling of going crazy. Maybe this is true for you, too. Or, you could be afraid that someone else you love will die, or you are afraid of your own mortality. This can make you feel vulnerable and make it hard to concentrate or sleep well.

The solution is to take away some of the giant's power. The only way to do this is to talk about your fears. To pull them out of the bundle one by one and express how you feel about them. Talk with someone who is understanding and supportive. That could be a friend, counselor, sibling, parent, coworker, or support group member. By exposing your fears, they tend to shrink and solutions begin to come to mind.

Perhaps all the dragons in our lives are princesses who are only waiting to see us act, just once, with beauty and courage. Perhaps everything that frightens us is, in its deepest essence, something helpless that wants our love.

~ Rainer Maria Rilke

There's a chance you won't feel like talking. You might think that by ignoring your feelings or staying busy that they won't catch up with you. Some grieving people even become prisoners in their own homes. They repress their anxiety, panic, and fear only to discover that these feelings are now repressing them. Don't let this happen to you. If the giant is barring your door, break it down through communication and sharing. Express it. Get it out. Write, talk, cry, lament, scream, and talk again. And if you are having symptoms of anxiety and panic attacks, see your medical doctor.

Remember that fear, too, passes. As you gain strength, mourn, and find answers as best you can, the giant will lose its power.

Many people wrongly exclude fear from the definition of courage, believing that courage is the absence of fear. … The reality, though, is that courage is fearful. When we are acting courageously, we are, most typically, very afraid. But we don't allow the fear we're carrying to stop us. Instead, we press on. This is the signature feature of courage: to carry on despite being fearful. Fear, thus, is an essential element in the definition of courage.

~ Bill Treasurer

Personal Reflection on Courage

Which fear is most prominent in my mind, today? What are some truths that counter this fear? What are some actions that challenge this fear? Who can I talk to about this fear? If there are no aspects of fear that are a part of my grief journey, what feelings am I most experiencing?

_____

_____

_____

_____

_____

_____

_____

_____

_____

Day 10

Feed Your Inner Flame

Do not let your fire go out, spark by irreplaceable spark, in the hopeless swamps of the approximate, the not-quite, the not-yet, the not-at-all. Do not let the hero in your soul perish, in lonely frustration for the life you deserved, but have never been able to reach. Check your road and the nature of your battle.

~ Ayn Rand

In each and every one of us burns a divine spark—a life force that is uniquely ours. This inner flame radiates our passions, our uniqueness, our inner being out into the world. It is the "us" others see when they look into our eyes or listen to our deepest, most intimate thoughts. It is the "you" revealed.

Some think of their divine spark as their soul—the part that connects them to all other living creatures, to the earth, and to God. Others see the divine spark as an aura that glows and reveals our spirits. Still others see it as the part of us that is from the whole, the divine, the positive, loving undercurrent that feeds all life. However you care to describe it, your divine spark is yours to guard and feed. Without it, you are at risk of feeling hopeless and disconnected.

Find a way to feed your inner flame. Maybe that involves going to a place of worship, having a heart-to-heart with your best friend, meditating, reading poetry or philosophy, listening to music, creating art, writing, seeing a therapist, or being in nature.

When you love someone and he dies, your inner flame gets muted by sadness and grief. Your loss may even extinguish your zest for life and your hope for the future. When you feel muted, you may need to turn your life over to others for care. Through your connection with others, your flame will reignite. You will eventually find the fortitude to continue on. Being willing to ask for help takes courage.

What lies behind us and what lies before us are tiny matters compared to what lies within us.

~ Ralph Waldo Emerson

Courage is not the absence of fear, but rather the judgment that something else is more important than fear.

~ Meg Cabot

Consider creating a sacred mourning space to use privately to feed your flame and give your spark a chance to burn, unfettered. Maybe there's a favorite spot in nature—a rock or a tree perhaps—that speaks to your spirit. Or maybe it is a special place in your house—a space where you feel closer to your loved one or a bench in your garden. Have the fortitude to use this sacred place, dedicated exclusively to the needs of your soul, to contemplate your life and your loss. The word contemplate literally means "to create space for the divine to enter."

Another way to keep your flame burning is to start each day with a meaningful meditation or prayer. For many mourners, waking up is the hardest part of the day. Even something simple, as in: "Thank you, God, for this day," can help restart your spark and create a self-compassionate, gentle, loving start to your day.

Take a moment to consider what activities give you clarity and peace, and a feeling of being centered. Make a vow to take these actions as often as you can.

Personal Reflection on Courage

How do I feel about my "divine spark" right now? If I am aware that my divine spark has been muted or extinguished, what can I do to help myself see some light in the midst of the dark? What can I do in the future to increase my inner flame?

_____

_____

_____

_____

_____

_____

_____

_____

_____

_____

_____

_____

Day 11

Be Uncomfortable

To suppress grief, the pain, is to condemn oneself to a living death. Living fully means being completely one with what you are experiencing and not holding it at arm's length.

~ Philip Kapleau

It requires more courage to suffer than to die.

~ Napoleon Bonaparte

As Carl Jung observed, "There is no coming to consciousness without pain." Feeling your pain can be uncomfortable. It is tempting to turn away and ignore it. After all, who wants to feel bad? Who wants to hurt?

It's a common misconception that we should avoid the painful parts of grief. Society encourages us to move away from grief rather than toward it. Grief is seen as something to get over rather than experience. Unfortunately, grief will not be ignored, and cannot reconcile on its own. The pain of grief will continue to try to get your attention until you have the courage to open to its presence, in small doses over time. Ironically, moving away from your pain only creates more pain. I've seen this over and over again as I've companioned people through grief. You see, if we shut our heart to pain, we also shut it to love.

Of course, sometimes you will feel a need to "buck up"—at work, during a business meeting, when shopping and in other public places. Yet you can resist the urge to avoid your pain by giving yourself ample private time. In other words, instead of going to the coffee shop on Saturday to surf the Net and hang out, do it at home; likewise for roaming the stores in search of distraction or always working late. Some of this is fine. You know when you've reached your limit with pain and need a break. But when you feel yourself getting itchy and irritable, stop and listen. It is probably your pain wanting a chance to

Don't get discouraged; it is often the last
key in the bunch that opens the lock.

~ Unknown

It's not the load that breaks you down;
it's the way you carry it.

~ Lena Horne

speak. Reject the American idea that "tears do no good," and that pain should be avoided at all costs, and instead welcome the pain. Even muck about with it.

Create time to mourn openly and honestly, even when it feels uncomfortable. If you are involved in several organizations, cut down to one or two. If you can afford it, hire someone to clean your house or care for your lawn. Start a new habit of quiet activities, like taking baths, nightly walks, or limiting your television watching to one or two shows a day. Set a conscious intention to open to grief and allow grief to speak. Your grief is like a wound; it needs soothing, space, and time to heal. When you can, gently remove the bandage and give your pain fresh air.

Yes, it takes courage to be uncomfortable, especially when you are with others who are uncomfortable with your grief. During this healing time, limit your engagements with these types of people. Instead, find people who are not afraid to walk with you through grief, who are not afraid to see you cry, wail, rage, or act otherwise unpredictably.

Personal Reflection on Courage

How do I avoid, or put off, the pain of grief? What habit can I change to create time to befriend my pain? Who are the people in my life who allow me to express my pain and don't try to fix me?

Day 12

Reach Out When You're in Trouble

*I beg you to take courage; the brave
soul can mend even disaster.*

~ Catherine II

*Refusing to ask for help when you need it is
refusing someone the chance to be helpful.*

~ Ric Ocasek

A friend is a gift you give yourself.

~ Robert Louis Stevenson

I'm lucky. When disaster strikes I have a few good friends whom I can call and tell anything, without fear of judgment or shock. I know that no matter what I do or say, they will love me regardless. This, I know, is a precious, rare gift. If you do not have a person like this in your life right now, know that you can find one. You need someone who will take your call in the darkest of hours.

Being able to mourn out loud to someone helps release the pressure valve that's threatening to blow inside of you. It offers a sane perspective at seemingly insane moments. The thought of going on without your loved one may seem unbearable, and finding someone to share that heartbreak with makes it somewhat fathomable, at least for a while.

Hearing a friend's kind words of support and love is like a rope thrown overboard when you are drowning. All you have to do is hold on and let them pull you up. True friends will do this for you. And this act of giving and receiving only strengthens your friendship and your pact to be there for each other no matter what. Those who really care about you want to hear from you. They want to provide comfort and support. Trust this.

Do you have a friend or relative like this? Someone who has your back no matter what? Who is dedicated to listen and support versus advise and instruct? You might and you don't even know it. Tragedies and deaths have a way of making people either

You can build walls all the way to the sky and I will find a way to fly above them. You can try to pin me down with a hundred thousand arms, but I will find a way to resist. And there are many of us out there, more than you think.... People who love in a world without walls, people who love into hate, into refusal, against hope, and without fear.

~ Lauren Oliver

Losing love is like a window into your heart; Everybody sees you're blown apart; Everybody sees the wind blow....

~ Paul Simon

scatter or step forward. Sometimes it's your longtime friend who turns away while a mere acquaintance reaches out. Take the hand of the person who is reaching out to you, even if you don't know her well. If she is reaching out, most likely she has the fortitude to pull you up.

If there isn't someone in your life currently who can provide an empathetic, non-judging ear, you'll need to go out and find one. Here are some ideas: join a grief support group, talk with the leader of your place of worship, or find a professional counselor. Better yet, create a network of people to call. Do you know someone else who has experienced a death that is similar to the one you have experienced? Those who have lived through loss know it best. Hearing people tell their stories of grief and pain in a support group is incredibly powerful, and helps you know you are not alone. Check your local hospice or hospital for grief support groups.

Sharing your pain with others won't make it go away, but it will, over time, make it more bearable. Reaching out for help is reaching out for love. By letting a friend carry some of your grief, you will have the strength to go on.

Personal Reflection on Courage

Who is your go-to person when emotional disaster strikes? Who else can you add to your list of supporters? Have you been isolating? If so, what can you do to reach out for help?

_____

_____

_____

_____

_____

_____

_____

_____

_____

_____

_____

_____

_____

Day 13

Take the Next Small Step

The only courage that matters is the kind that gets you from one moment to the next.

~ Mignon McLaughlin

A hero is no braver than an ordinary man, but he is braver five minutes longer.

~ Ralph Waldo Emerson

The journey of a thousand miles must begin with a single step.

~ Lao Tzu

When you are facing a challenge or living in grief, the whole picture is too much to take in all at once. Do what's in front of you today. That's all. And what that is will depend on where you are in your grief journey, the circumstances of the death, and how close you were with the person who died, among other factors. Maybe that small step is simply getting out of bed and getting yourself to work. Maybe it is picking up the phone and asking a friend to meet you for coffee, or saying yes when someone asks if he can help. Later, a small step might be walking through the doors of a support group, or setting an appointment with a counselor. Or, it might be allowing yourself to sit in your wound and actively mourn.

At times, you will have to act in the face of resistance. Grief can weigh you down. If you have an overwhelming urge to isolate from others, make yourself connect. If guilt and anger dominate your days, tell a trusted friend or counselor. If you don't see any reason to go on and all you can feel is doom, force yourself to do something uplifting.

Sometimes, simply taking care of your physical self can make you feel better. Get good sleep, eat healthy foods, exercise. Exercise has been proven to decrease depression as much as prescription medication in some studies. So even if your body feels like lead, get on your bike and pedal around the neighborhood. Also, be gentle with yourself. You are allowed breaks from pain! Ask a friend or coworker to accompany you to a funny movie, play a silly game or watch YouTube videos on your iPad, or get lost in a good book. It also takes fortitude to take care of yourself and trust your intuition—that still, wise place inside you that, like a level, signals when you are not centered.

I urge you to be bold as you go through your day. Do the next, hard, right thing that's in front of you. If the phone rings, answer it. If the tears come, let them flow. If grief has you pinned down, do something light and enjoyable.

Personal Reflection on Courage

What small opportunities for healing presented themselves to you today? Did you take them? Can you see a way to take them next time?

_____

_____

_____

_____

_____

_____

Day 14

Breathe

Sometimes even to live is an act of courage.

~ Lucius Annaeus Seneca

Courage is the price that life exacts for granting peace.

~ Amelia Earhart

As you experience your grief and acknowledge your need to authentically mourn, remember to simply breathe. The benefits of deep breathing are physical, emotional, and spiritual. With each breath, you allow yourself to open, take in, and then release.

Breathing invites your body into a more relaxed physical state, creates more restful sleep, lowers your blood pressure, increases oxygen circulation, improves your immune system, increases your ability to concentrate, calms your mind, and stimulates an overall feeling of well-being. Grief can naturally close you down, but breathing opens you up. The power of breath helps you begin to fill your empty spaces. The old wisdom of "count to ten" is all about taking a breath to open up space for something to happen. The lovely paradox is that in slowing down, you create divine momentum to move forward in your journey through grief.

The death of someone precious to you changes your entire way of life. Naturally, this can be overwhelming and create fear and anxiety. With fear and anxiety come tightness, tension, and shallow breathing—the withholding of life. This can trigger your instincts to either speed up, flee, or hold on tight. If you feel yourself wanting to speed up, you may be better served to slow down. If you breathe deeply, your body will naturally slow down. If you feel the need to flee, you may be better served to face what you need to face. If you feel the need to hold on

Promise me you'll always remember: You're braver than you believe, and stronger than you seem, and smarter than you think.

~ A. A. Milne

tight, you may be better served to surrender to what you need to experience. Taking deep breaths during these times can help you befriend your fear and anxiety.

Right this moment, please take five full minutes to focus only on your breathing. Imagine that you're inhaling the spiritual energy you need to help you integrate this loss into your life and that you're exhaling your feelings of sadness and grief. No, this doesn't make your grief go away, nor should it. But it does help you soothe your soul and discover some light in the midst of darkness. You may even rediscover the joy of being alive.

So, what does this have to do with courage? You activate your innate courage little by little, breath by breath. Just a few minutes of deep breathing each day will provide you a lovely spiritual perspective on where you are in your journey through grief and through life.

Personal Reflection on Courage

After you have completed the five full minutes of focused breathing, write about what the experience was like for you. How will you integrate deep breathing into the days to come?

_____

_____

_____

_____

_____

_____

_____

_____

_____

_____

_____

_____

_____

Day 15

Act As If

The bravest thing you can do when you are not brave is to profess courage and act accordingly.

~ Corra Harris

Courage is grace under pressure.

~ Ernest Hemingway

You might be familiar with this saying; the purpose of "acting as if" is to get you moving, despite a lack of confidence or belief that you can do what you want to do, or be who you want to be. For example, if you can't imagine showing up at work, act as if you have the strength to do so. Or, if your partner has died and you can't fathom handling the finances or home repairs on your own, act as if you know what you are doing.

The goal isn't false bravado. The goal is simply to give you that edge of self-assurance that you need to enter into a seemingly daunting task. Often what happens is that once you walk into that office or explore that finance software or read about how to patch that wall, you realize that indeed, you can do it.

When someone you love dies, your life often gets rearranged. Maybe the death means a new home, a new way to spend holidays, or a refocus of priorities. All this change is an opportunity for growth, and growth means exploring your assumptions about life and using your potential. What you consider valuable today may be different than before. Maybe you are asking yourself, "Why did I spend so much time at work?" or "Why didn't we ever go out dancing, ride in a hot air balloon, or climb that mountain together?" It's natural that you rethink your values and priorities. You may even be redefining yourself by asking questions, like "Who am I? What am I meant to do with my life?" Until you make peace with

Believe you can and you're halfway there.

~ Theodore Roosevelt

I believe that the most important single thing, beyond discipline and creativity, is daring to dare.

~ Maya Angelou

your purpose and use your potential, you may not experience contentment or true joy.

Embrace the change at hand. Change means having to face new situations, develop new skills, and polish new strengths. If you can't muster up the personal power to tackle the change, try acting as if. Another way to think about acting as if is "fake it till you make it." To act as if, literally pretend you are someone with confidence and "play act" the scene in real time. You may feel like a fake at first, but that's OK. When you act as if, real confidence evolves from mock confidence and becomes your new reality.

A good way to act as if is to create meaningful declarations. For example, you might say, "I will survive, and I will discover my strengths," or "My life will be full and happy once again," or "I have the courage to live on my own and redefine my life." If we put an intention out there, and contemplate it enough times, it usually starts to manifest.

> *Courage is very important. Like a*
> *muscle, it is strengthened by use.*
> ~ Ruth Gordon

Personal Reflection on Courage

Write down a number of declarations—things you would like to be true in your life. Say them boldly out loud, even if you can't imagine making them happen.

_____

_____

_____

_____

_____

_____

_____

_____

_____

_____

_____

_____

_____

_____

Day 16

Bushwhack Your Own Path

Do not go where the path may lead; go instead where there is no path and leave a trail.

~ Ralph Waldo Emerson

I learned that courage was not the absence of fear, but the triumph over it. The brave man is not he who does not feel afraid, but he who conquers that fear.

~ Nelson Mandela

In life, everyone grieves, but no two grief journeys are the same. I like to envision grief as a wilderness—a deep, dark forest. Your walk through the wilderness might be rocky or smooth. You might climb boulders or find inspiration in the moonrise. You'll find places of personal meaning that will forever change you. And you will, I promise, find your own way, as long as you stay aware and awake to what you encounter along the way.

"What makes my grief unique?" you may ask. Many things influence what your wilderness will be like and how profound, difficult, or relatively smooth your journey may be. Here are a few to consider from my book *Understanding Your Grief: Ten Essential Touchstones for Finding Hope and Healing Your Heart*:

- Your relationship with the person who died
- The circumstances of the death
- The ritual or funeral experience
- The people in your life
- Your unique personality
- The unique personality of the person who died
- Your gender
- Your cultural, religious, and spiritual background
- Other crises or stresses in your life
- Your past experience with loss and death
- Your physical health

There is a stubbornness about me that never can bear to be frightened at the will of others. My courage always rises at every attempt to intimidate me.

~ Jane Austen

Listen to the people who love you. Believe that they are worth living for even when you don't believe it. Be brave; be strong.... Exercise because it's good for you even if every step weighs a thousand pounds. Eat when food itself disgusts you. Reason with yourself when you have lost your reason.

~ Andrew Solomon

I do not say that your grief is unique to make you feel alone. On the contrary, I believe it is extremely important to connect with others who have walked the path of grief and mourning before you. To ultimately heal, you must be touched by the experiences of others—people who can offer you true comfort and hope for the future. You will draw understanding and strength from the similarities in your journeys.

Yet it's valuable to know that you and you alone get to decide what your journey will be like. You get to determine the pace; you get to choose what kind of interactions or support works best; and you get to define your experience, rather than becoming a victim to common misconceptions about grief and mourning, including these oldies but goodies:

- Grief and mourning progress in a predictable order.
- Grief should be avoided. Stay busy!
- Tears are a sign of weakness.
- Always thinking about the person who died is pathological.
- Being upset and openly mourning means you are weak in faith.
- It's best to get over your grief as quickly as possible.
- Your grief and mourning will eventually end.

These misconceptions are not only false, they send a dangerous message—a message to deny your feelings and avoid your grief. They do not offer true relief or transformation, only a promise of becoming stuck.

Remember this above all: There are no rules on how you should grieve and mourn. If you want to scream and wail night after night, do it. If you want to quietly grieve as you write in a journal or read poetry, do it. It's your path, and you hold the machete. Bushwhack.

Personal Reflection on Courage

What does your grief journey look like? What are your unique needs? What are some new truths that you are discovering along the way?

_____

_____

_____

_____

_____

_____

_____

_____

_____

_____

Day 17

Stop and Rest

Come to me, all you who are weary and burdened, and I will give you rest.

~ Matthew 11:28

Mourning takes a lot of work. You may feel exhausted and have low energy a lot lately. This is extremely common. Your body is simply telling you that you need a lot of rest. Feeling so many emotions is extremely tiring.

Make sure you are getting plenty of sleep, at least eight hours if possible. If you find it hard to sleep, try establishing some relaxing bedtime habits. Read a book with low light instead of watching television, take a bath, or spend a few minutes meditating on your day and releasing tasks through writing or an outward declaration that you can "get to that tomorrow." Try sleep-promoting supplements like melatonin, valerian, or St. John's Wort (which may also reduce symptoms of depression). If your bed is uncomfortable, replace it or get a new, good pillow.

Also, allow yourself to nap during the day. If you are not used to taking daytime naps, tell yourself that you need, and deserve, this time to rejuvenate. While you sleep and catnap, your mind sorts out dilemmas you may be mulling over. You might awake from a dream feeling more integrated, centered, and satisfied. Take a moment to write your dream down; it may offer insight that will help you on your grief journey.

Resting also involves setting grief aside and doing something enjoyable or something that doesn't take much thought or energy. Maybe that's reading an entertaining magazine,

Courage doesn't always roar. Sometimes courage is the little voice at the end of the day that says I'll try again tomorrow.

~ Mary Anne Radmacher

sunbathing, or simply closing your eyes and listening to the sounds of nature or music.

You cannot do all your grieving and mourning all at once. That is too much to take in. Allow yourself to "dose" the pain. In other words, feel it in small waves, then allow it to retreat until you feel the fortitude to take on the next wave. Realize what a big task active grieving and mourning are, and be gentle with yourself. Have realistic expectations. For example, your grief will probably hurt more before it hurts less. Your grief will be unpredictable. Your grief will not go away if you ignore it. Lastly, you can't grieve alone. You need the help of others.

Keep in mind that while grieving comes naturally, mourning is more of a conscious effort. To mourn, you embrace your grief, really explore it and feel it, then release it physically through words, crying, actions, and rituals. This is hard work. After a session of mourning, allow yourself to rest and retreat. Resting will give you the courage to mourn again tomorrow.

Personal Reflection on Courage

Make a list of activities that make you feel calm and rested.
Vow to do a few every day.

_____

_____

_____

_____

_____

_____

_____

_____

_____

_____

_____

_____

_____

Day 18

Actively Mourn

Don't be afraid of your fears. They're not there to scare you. They're there to let you know that something is worth it.

~ C. JoyBell C.

I wanted you to see what real courage is..... It's when you know you're licked before you begin, but you begin anyway and see it through no matter what.

~ Atticus Finch

I've talked a lot about active mourning and how it is important to express your grief—to release it outwardly rather than only feeling it inwardly. Yet you might be left wondering what active mourning really looks like. In the end, only you can determine what mourning is for you, but here are some ideas to get you started. They will help you actively embrace your grief and express the pain of your separation:

- Seeing photos of your loved one can help you integrate your loss. Sit down and go through photo albums by yourself or with someone who loves you. Recount the memories as you look at pictures of time spent with your loved one. Or, display photos somewhere prominent. In the first weeks, you may want to keep the photo display intact from the funeral (if you created one) in your home so you can visit it throughout the day. Also, pull photos out during the holidays. Some people even leave a place at the dinner table for their loved one who has died, with a picture to represent his or her presence.

- Use a "linking object" to help you process your loss. I once counseled a widow who found it comforting to sleep with her husband's shirt. This is a perfectly normal response to wanting to hold on to a tangible, physical expression of a person. Another woman had inherited her mother's jewelry box and decided to wear a piece of her jewelry every day. She said it made her feel like she was taking

A ship is safe in harbor, but that's not what ships are for.
~ William G.T. Shedd

The only courage that matters is the kind that gets you from one moment to the next.
~ Mignon McLaughlin

her mother with her into her day. I often wear my father's watch that he passed down to me just before his death. It's okay to hold on to some of your loved one's belongings as long as you need.

- Visit places that hold special significance, places that stimulate memories of times shared together. Walk a favorite footpath or go to a favorite restaurant, coffee shop, or bookstore.

- Have a ritual or ceremony. You can light candles and invite a few special people who also loved the person to join in on passing a candle and sharing a memory. You can do this or another ritual as often as needed. Other ideas: plant a tree or flowering bush, or build a sacred shrine of the loved one's favorite items or pictures of cherished times.

I'd be remiss not to mention that sometimes memories are not pleasant. If this is true for you, mourning can be difficult. Try to share your painful and ambivalent memories with a trusted person in your life. If you repress difficult memories, you risk carrying an underlying sadness or anger into your future. Remember, active mourning takes courage. Be brave and don't turn away.

Personal Reflections on Courage

What are three ways I can actively mourn? When in the next week can I carry out one of these ideas?

_____

_____

_____

_____

_____

_____

_____

_____

_____

_____

_____

_____

_____

_____

Day 19

Invite Mystery

Let mystery have its place in you; do not be always turning up your whole soil with the ploughshare of self-examination, but leave a little fallow corner in your heart ready for any seed the winds may bring...

~ Henri Frederic Amiel

Mystery is a resource, like coal or gold, and its preservation is a fine thing.

~ Tim Cahill

Be open to the mystery, or what some call the universe, sending answers to your questions or gifts of comfort. I once counseled a woman who was grieving for her husband. She wasn't sure she believed in an afterlife, but the strangest thing kept happening. She started seeing foxes everywhere, on the bike path near her house, in the store parking lot, even on the night of his death, right before she received the news. You see, her husband had a special appreciation for foxes. Maybe this was all coincidence, maybe not. In the end it didn't really matter. Seeing the foxes gave her comfort. Through these experiences she felt a mysterious connection to the person who died. Throughout the years, whenever she saw a fox she felt uplifted. Many others have shared similar "mystical experiences" with me, often saying they've felt the presence of their loved one near.

Most mourners whom I've companioned through grief are comforted by the belief that somehow, somewhere, the spirit of the person who died lives on. In grief, we often wish that we had just one more chance to communicate. If you feel this way, then invite your loved one's spirit to sit down beside you and listen to what you have to say. It's important to release these words. Saying them will give you some relief from your pain. It's hard to separate from a loved one, and carrying on a relationship with the person who died is natural. In the words of famous playwright Robert Benchley, "Death ends a life, not a relationship."

*Here is the world. Beautiful and terrible
things will happen. Don't be afraid.*

~ Frederick Buechner

*Have enough courage to trust love one more
time and always one more time.*

~ Maya Angelou

I urge you to invite the mystery. If the person who died adored birds, hang bird feeders everywhere. If she loved to sit in the middle of an aspen grove and watch the light play on the leaves, do that for her—and invite her to join you. There is no guarantee she will, but you will find it healing to embrace the mystery of the unknown and to honor her spirit.

Another way to invite mystery is to open your heart and mind to new ways of being in the world. Grief changes you. It can strip you down and make you feel vulnerable. Yet this stripping down also leaves you feeling humble and open. It's a strange starting over, a new beginning. If you feel this openness, I urge you to take the next good opportunity for change and growth that presents itself. It may call for you to think in a way you've never thought before, or do something brand new. Do it, despite possible hesitation or fear. This is courage in action. It takes tenacity to step into the unknown and trust that you will be able to find your way. And you will, as long as you stay committed to moving forward. If it helps, imagine the person you love walking beside you, urging you on.

Personal Reflection on Courage

What mystery can I invite into my life today? What opportunity
is inviting me to enter the unknown? What comes to mind when
I reflect on the words, "Mystery is something to be pondered,
not explained"?

_____

_____

_____

_____

_____

_____

_____

_____

_____

_____

_____

Day 20

Be Mindful

The most fundamental aggression to ourselves, the most fundamental harm we can do to ourselves, is to remain ignorant by not having the courage and the respect to look at ourselves honestly and gently.

~ Pema Chödrön

Don't believe everything you think. Thoughts are just that—thoughts.

~ Allan Lokos

Most likely, you are familiar with the term "mindfulness." It's a popular idea these days. A recent Amazon search came up with more than 3,000 books on the topic. I am not going to try to stake a claim to the word, but I do like how it fits with my idea of conscious grieving. Being mindful—or present and attentive—to your grief will help you move through it and reshape it.

Mindfulness is being fully alert and aware of the moment— your thoughts, your physical sensations, your emotions, your surroundings. I like to think of mindfulness as consciously, and forgivingly, acknowledging what you are thinking and feeling. To actively mourn, you need to know what you are thinking and feeling, so you can act versus react, or heal versus simply feeling bad.

At quiet moments, take time to stop and watch your thoughts and feelings walk across your mind. Observe. Take notes. See them as separate entities that have stepped into your mind, and watch where they go and what they become. Don't stop them in their tracks by thinking, "That's stupid" or, "What's wrong with me," or "I shouldn't be angry (or sad, anxious, worried, scared, etc.)." Just let your thoughts or feelings run their course and think, "Hmmm, interesting." If it helps, imagine you are with a white-bearded, benevolent, supportive therapist sitting back comfortably and rubbing his chin. He listens without judging and only wants to help you gain insight and heal.

It stands to reason that anyone who learns to live well will die well. The skills are the same: being present in the moment, and humble, and brave, and keeping a sense of humor.

~ Victoria Moran

The secret of happiness is freedom; the secret of freedom is courage.

~ Carrie Jones

You might be surprised by what comes up. You might hear the voice of a judge who comments negatively. Don't object. Just listen. Take on the "Hmmm, interesting" stance. He is only giving you information about yourself and what you may need. For example, the judge might say: "You are weak!" or, "Life is awful and there is no reason to live." If so, then you know what you are up against. You can choose how to respond. You can take action to counter the judge's claims. For example, you can consciously choose affirmations that proclaim the opposite and do things that make you feel strong and able.

Being mindful of your feelings will help you "sit in your wound." By experiencing your feelings, rather than turning away, you will integrate your grief—you will own it, rather than it owning you. When you don't acknowledge your feelings, you might experience the unsettledness and agitation they tend to create on the surface rather than the real and raw emotion underneath. These emotions may be hard to feel, but welcome them as best you can.

There is a saying that declares, "Our thoughts are prayers." This simply means that what you think about most of the time is what you wish to bring forth in your life. Your thoughts make up your intentions. You get to choose what you want to manifest.

Personal Reflection on Courage

What am I thinking about, or praying for, these days? Are most of my thoughts life-affirming? Or are they working against me?

_____

_____

_____

_____

_____

_____

_____

_____

_____

_____

_____

_____

Day 21

Set Your Compass

Obstacles are those frightful things you see when you take your eyes off your goals.

~ Henry Ford

The most courageous act is still to think for yourself. Aloud.

~ Coco Chanel

You have probably heard the phrase, "Live with intention." What does this mean, and how does it relate to your grief? "Intention" is defined as "a course of action that one intends to follow, an aim, a purpose." Living with intention, then, simply means making a conscious choice about what you want to experience. In regards to grief, if you set your intention to heal, you are committing, on all levels, to be positively changed by your grief rather than oppressed by the weight of it.

I am not advocating that you "keep your chin up" during your grief process—not in the least. Keeping your chin up means denying your feelings, which makes grief a heavy load—one you may never be able to set down. Rather, I want you to welcome your feelings of grief, to ask for support when you need it, to allow yourself the time and attention you need to grieve and mourn, and to consciously take on a belief that you will survive. In other words, I urge you to actively guide your grief, to choose what your grief journey will look like.

Setting your compass, or intention, also means making your outer reality match your inner thoughts and beliefs. When you become aware of your inner thoughts and beliefs, you can influence your reality. So, take a moment and set your intention to heal through grief. Intentions can be set in prayer, said out loud to a supportive person, or written in a journal. Your intentions might include a version of the following:

Whatever you do, you need courage. Whatever course you decide upon, there is always someone to tell you that you are wrong. There are always difficulties arising that tempt you to believe your critics are right. To map out a course of action and follow it to an end requires…courage…

~ Ralph Waldo Emerson

Your time is limited, so don't waste it living someone else's life. Don't be trapped by dogma—which is living with the results of other people's thinking. Don't let the noise of others' opinions drown out your own inner voice. And most important, have the courage to follow your heart and intuition.

~ Steve Jobs

- I can and will survive this time.
- I will not turn away from the pain of my loss.
- When I am struggling, I will ask for help.
- When I am avoiding my grief and getting irritable or depressed, I will do something positive to regain the strength to face it.
- I will take care of myself and be gentle with myself during this time.
- I alone will decide what my grief journey will look like, and I will honor my unique needs.
- I will have the courage and strength to make it through each day.

Now, close your eyes and see your future self. See yourself feeling joy and living fully. Maybe you are laughing with a friend or feeling serene alone in nature. Imagine you are thinking of the person who died, and, while you still miss him or her and the pain is still there, it no longer crushes you. You also feel your loved one's spirit hovering above, finding satisfaction that you are living a full life.

Set your intentions, and let them guide the choices you make and beliefs you adopt as you grieve and mourn. Feel your strength and inner determination. It is there, along with hope, waiting to come forth.

Personal Reflection on Courage

Take a minute and write a few intentions about your grief process. Which intentions will direct you through your grief rather than around it?

_____

_____

_____

_____

_____

_____

_____

_____

_____

_____

_____

_____

_____

Day 22

Get Real

Courage is what it takes to stand up and speak;
courage is also what it takes to sit down and listen.

~ Winston Churchill

When someone you love dies, you "get real" real quick. You instantly realize what is important in life. You realize that the people you love, and your relationship with them, are at the top of your list. You also wake up to what you value in life and what brings your life meaning. Maybe that's spending time with loved ones, really connecting with people, living life to the fullest, sharing joy, being kind, helping others, attending church or another place of worship, experiencing nature, going on adventures, or making the world a better place through volunteering. Whatever you find valuable and meaningful in life, do it as much as possible. Being real and doing what matters strengthen your resolve and faith. They bring purpose back into your life.

When hope seems absent, open your heart—your well of reception—and find that faith sustains you. When you are able to find what is good, what is sweet, what is tender in life, despite the deep, overwhelming pain of your loss, you will feel hope for the future and faith that you will survive this time. Surrounding yourself with meaning fortifies your spirit and gives you the strength to go on.

If you are spiritual, feel the confidence that God or a higher power is with you in your grief and that you are being carried when you feel weak and hopeless. Also, feel faith in humanity—in the goodness of others—and let that faith carry you when your journey gets hard.

My great hope is to laugh as much as I cry; to get my work done and try to love somebody and have the courage to accept their love in return.

~ Maya Angelou

Being real will demand slowing down and allowing times of silence. It will require you to stay put when you feel a rush of painful memories or emotions. It is healthy and necessary for you to remember the person who died. Your mind and spirit may need to process memories over and over again. You may experience griefbursts—sudden, overwhelming moments of missing the person you loved and crying or sobbing. As best you can, accept these griefbursts and allow the deep pain to wash over you. Wail, sob, and scream as needed. Afterwards, talk with someone who cares about you.

If you commit to being real and staying in touch with your grief and also doing things that really matter, you will reconcile your grief. You will pass from this painful time and someday feel joy and a belief in life and what it has to offer once again.

Personal Reflection on Courage

What brings your life meaning? Name ten things that you really care about and value.

_____

_____

_____

_____

_____

_____

_____

_____

_____

_____

_____

_____

_____

_____

Day 23

Say No

I say yes when I mean no and the wrinkle grows.

~ Naomi Shihab Nye

A vital part of self-care when you are experiencing grief is exercising the courage to say no.

Think of it this way: Grieving may be the hardest work you have ever done. It requires lots of energy. Especially soon after the death, you may lack the energy as well as the desire to participate in activities you used to find pleasurable.

Befriend the courage that is within you to say no when you're asked to do something that you really don't want—or don't have the energy—to do right now. Don't allow yes to slip off your tongue before you have discernment about what you are committing yourself to! Squelching the courage to say no can result in a calendar full of obligations to people and activities that don't really enrich your life right now.

Remember—you have some special needs in grief, and you do not have to take on commitments that leave you feeling stressed, run-down, and exhausted. Your natural lethargy of grief is telling you to not place too many demands on yourself.

Ask yourself: Is anything overburdening me right now? Do any friends or family have inappropriate expectations of me? Do I have any inappropriate expectations of myself right now? Are people attempting to get me to go out into the world in ways I'm not ready for at this time in my journey?

Have the courage to act instead of react.

~ Oliver Wendell Holmes

If you can rid yourself of any extraneous burdens, you will have more time to mourn, which in turn will eventually encourage you to go back out into the world.

When you say yes to any demand, request, or condition that is contrary to your soul's nature, the price you pay is that your divine spark is muted. Despite the instinct to want to comply with the requests of well-meaning people around you, keep in mind that your soul will grow even more weary when you engage in activities that, for now, are inherently against your nature.

Only by understanding why you should say no will you find the necessary courage, when the time comes, to say yes. Realize you cannot keep saying no forever. There will always be those firsts that, even though they may be difficult, will need to be attended—that first wedding, that first birthday party, that first christening, etc. after the death. So, while it will take courage to say no right now, it will also take courage to begin to step back out into the world and embrace some of life's most joyous moments.

Personal Reflection on Courage

Make a list of all the optional events and commitments that feel like a burden to you right now. Next to each item, write down how you will relieve yourself of it, at least temporarily.

_____

_____

_____

_____

_____

_____

_____

_____

_____

_____

_____

_____

_____

_____

Day 24

Try on Your Loved One's Shoes

Courage is the ladder on which all the other virtues mount.

~ Clare Booth Luce

The stories of past courage can define that ingredient—they can teach, they can offer hope, they can provide inspiration. But they cannot supply courage itself. For this each man must look into his own soul.

~ John F. Kennedy

There is no better way to honor the person who died than to explore what mattered to her or emulate her strongest characteristics. Take inventory, right now, of her being. Who was she, in her finest moments? What did she value? What were her strengths? Which traits did she admire in other people? What was she like when she was young? What were her political, moral, and religious values? Which activities did she enjoy doing? What were some of her favorite landscapes, animals, cities, places? Where was she most in her element? What did you admire most about her? What was her philosophy on life? Which mottos did she live by? Do you know her history?

Of course you know the person who died, but you might be surprised by the whole of who he was. Ask others who also loved this person to answer some of these questions. By exploring the person you love from many angles, you are essentially trying on his shoes. You are imagining what life was like to be him.

This exercise also helps you grieve. To remember how selfless or tenacious or caring your loved one was, your heart opens and you may feel an outpouring of love or a rush of empathy for this person. When your heart is open, you invite your grief to express itself.

Taking inventory of who your loved one was may also bring up feelings about times that weren't so great—or traits you

Let today be the day…you look for the good in everyone you meet and respect their journey.

~ Steve Maraboli

disliked about him. It is rare to love every aspect of a person. Everyone has room to grow, and everyone is a product of their upbringing, to some extent. We are all human. I am not advocating that you forgive every negative aspect of the person who died. Rather, I think to fully grieve you need to feel feelings of hurt along with feelings of love and admiration. If you don't, you risk placing this person on a pedestal and feeling guilty every time you remember something that challenges this placement. Yet death naturally softens hard times, and makes you view the person as a whole—good, bad, ugly, and beautiful.

It's nice to think about the person's highest self—in other words, who she really tried to be, even when she maybe didn't make it. What did she strive for? If she could have stripped away circumstances or characteristics that held her down, who could or would she have become?

Personal Reflection on Courage

Take a few minutes to review the life of the person who died—getting in touch with who he or she was, as a whole person. What did you most admire about him or her? Were there qualities or characteristics you didn't like?

_____

_____

_____

_____

_____

_____

_____

_____

_____

_____

_____

_____

Day 25

Manifest His or Her Spirit

Being deeply loved by someone gives you strength,
while loving someone deeply gives you courage.

~ Lao Tzu

Love is honesty. Love is a mutual respect for one another.

~ Simone Elkeles

Yesterday you explored every aspect of the person who died. Today, consider taking action to honor his highest self, his finest traits, or his greatest interests—to honor his spirit. Are there any unfinished dreams he had that you can bring about? Any causes you can contribute to that mattered to him? Any characteristics you can emulate?

Many people I have companioned find peace in honoring the person who died through action. There are millions of possibilities to do something—from simply making a commitment to practice one of her best traits (patience, kindness), to taking on one of her interests (bird-watching, tennis, reading), to making a positive change in your community, nation, or world. For example, if the person who died volunteered at a homeless shelter, you could carry on her work and also volunteer at a shelter. Or, if she was kind to strangers and always opened doors, smiled, and gave well wishes, you could try doing the same.

I know people who have organized or participated in fundraisers to raise money to find a cure for breast cancer, diabetes, and cystic fibrosis. Others have created college scholarships to help students earn a degree or seek a career held by the person who died. Thinking of something you want to do, however small or large, merely takes creativity and desire.

Success is not final, failure is not fatal: it is the courage to continue that counts.

~ Winston Churchill

I finally know the difference between pleasing and loving, obeying and respecting. It has taken me so many years to be okay with being different, and with being this alive, this intense.

~ Eve Ensler

It may help to keep something close at all times to remind you of what you want to manifest in the name of your loved one's spirit. Maybe it is a meaningful quote you've stuck to your fridge or computer, or a talisman you carry in your pocket—a coin, rock, or charm. Having something concrete to remind you of your goal will keep you moving toward it during busy days.

When you take action and live out life for the person who died, grief can come full circle. You will feel grief reconciling in your heart. Of course, you can't rush reconciliation by taking action, but along with active mourning, it can strengthen and fortify you. It can inspire you to live a full, meaningful life.

Imagine the person who died smiling down on you. Imagine he is pleased by what he sees—not only for the good deeds or actions you are carrying out in his name, but mostly for how it is transforming you, healing you, engaging you, and making you more whole. As you honor his soul, you are healing your own. Remember, grief work is soul work. Living your life with passion is the greatest testimony of love you can give.

Personal Reflection on Courage

What actions can I take to honor the spirit of the person who died? How can I best honor my loved one's life?

_____

_____

_____

_____

_____

_____

_____

_____

_____

_____

_____

_____

Day 26

Move Toward Reconciliation

Courage isn't having the strength to go on—it is going on when you don't have strength.

~ Napoleon Bonaparte

I like to use the term "reconcile" versus "resolve" when it comes to grief. Some authors speak of resolving, or recovering from, grief. To me, this implies an end to your grief. Through my work with thousands of grieving people, I know grief never distinctly ends. Know this now: You won't "get over" your grief.

Yet you will, someday, through intentional mourning, reconcile your grief. In other words, you will learn how to move forward without the physical presence of the person who died. You will realize that your life, however changed, is not only livable, but can also be enjoyable and meaningful. With reconciliation comes a renewed sense of energy and confidence. You will be able to acknowledge the death without it overwhelming you. The death and life of your loved one will become a tender part of you—sometimes felt with sadness, sometimes with joy and laughter.

The recipe for reconciling your grief is simple: walk your walk through the wilderness. Don't avoid steep slopes or knee-deep muck. Trust that someday you'll emerge from the darkness. Along the way, stop to talk, write, cry, think, play, paint, draw, work, act, or dance out your grief thoughts, worries, sadness, rage, joy, memories, fears, and pain. Doing so will keep you on your path toward reconciliation. Remember, you must descend into grief before you can transcend it.

At times the world may seem an unfriendly and sinister place, but believe that there is much more good in it than bad. All you have to do is look hard enough, and what might seem to be a series of unfortunate events may in fact be the first steps of a journey.

~ Lemony Snicket

Sometimes you will think you are out of the woods only to realize you need to return. Be open to whatever twists and turns your grief brings, and resist putting any kind of expectations or timeline on your journey.

You'll know that you are reaching reconciliation when memories and thoughts of the person who died are no longer so sharp and painful, or when griefbursts become less intense. Thoughts of your loved one will not dominate your mind all of the time. You'll catch yourself laughing and having fun—and this will feel okay. You will live fully in the present and look to the future rather than regret the past. Finally, you'll have a sense that you've survived.

Don't expect one great moment of arrival with reconciliation. Rather, you will more likely notice subtle changes and small advancements—like the way grass grows, a little at a time. When you feel growth, stop and have gratitude for it, no matter how small it seems. Carry hope and faith that you will, someday, reconcile your grief. As long as you valiantly walk the path set out for you, you'll reach reconciliation.

Personal Reflection on Courage

Am I open to whatever my walk through the wilderness of grief will bring? What can I do to further honor this walk?

_____

_____

_____

_____

_____

_____

_____

_____

_____

_____

_____

_____

_____

Day 27

Embrace a New Way of Being

For what it's worth: it's never too late or, in my case, too early to be whoever you want to be. There's no time limit, stop whenever you want. You can change or stay the same, there are no rules to this thing. We can make the best or the worst of it. I hope you make the best of it. And I hope you see things that startle you. I hope you feel things you never felt before. I hope you meet people with a different point of view. I hope you live a life you're proud of. If you find that you're not, I hope you have the strength to start all over again.

~ F. Scott Fitzgerald

When someone we love has died, we are forever changed. This makes sense. Those closest to us shape who we are. They help define us. When they are gone, to some degree we must reinvent ourselves.

Since your loved one has died, you may have discovered new attitudes or beliefs. Maybe you have gained insights that now influence how you live your life. You might also have developed new skills that you didn't need before, or taken on new work or a new career path, or even moved to a new area. Maybe you've even connected to new people.

Most likely, you have once again become familiar with your inner strengths and core personality traits. Some people find they return a bit to who they were before they knew the person who died. This is a comfortable thing to do—and provides opportunity to develop core characteristics in a new direction.

If you are actively grieving and mourning, you are growing. You are finding a new normal—a life without the physical presence of the person who died. If this resonates with you, take this opportunity to welcome this new way of being in the world. Give yourself the chance to rediscover what matters to you and what you enjoy doing. When you feel ready, challenge yourself by taking a class in something you always wanted to learn or traveling somewhere and visiting an old friend or a new place. Standing at the edge of a vast canyon, at the top

It takes courage to grow up and become who you really are.

~ e.e. cummings

of a mountain, or in the middle of the desert can put your life into perspective quickly.

I encourage you to question your assumptions about life. Take stock of your values. Look at your priorities. Most likely, you are doing this naturally.

Be careful to not fall into regret for not living this way earlier. For example, if you now believe that spending time with the people you love is the most important part of life, don't beat yourself up for the past when you didn't make spending time with the person who died a priority. Instead, imagine a time when you two were most connected, most happy. If he had been asked in that moment, what would your loved one have said that he'd want for you today? Or imagine his spirit, stripped down to pure love. No doubt, he would want you to feel more of that connection and happiness.

Allow yourself to live the life that you want. Fill it with happiness, connection, joy, and meaning. Feeling joy and having satisfaction in no way dishonors your grief or your loved one's memory. On the contrary, it validates it.

Personal Reflection on Courage

How has this death changed me? Which of these traits or beliefs do I want to enhance, and how can I do so?

_____

_____

_____

_____

_____

_____

_____

_____

_____

_____

_____

_____

_____

Day 28

Move with Purpose

Courage is very important. Like a muscle, it is strengthened by use.

~ Ruth Gordon

If I were asked to give what I consider the single most useful bit of advice for all humanity, it would be this: Expect trouble as an inevitable part of life and when it comes, hold your head high, look it squarely in eye and say, 'I will be bigger than you. You cannot defeat me.'

~ Ann Landers

Grieving and mourning is painful. It's hard to move toward pain. It takes a conscious effort to do so and demands courage. It would be much easier to deny your grief and bury it, going about your day as if it really didn't exist. Yet, like all pain, it will refuse to stay down. Maybe it will boil just below the surface and make you feel irritated, agitated, and crummy about life. Or maybe it will sit deep in your gut and weigh you down, making it hard to move, act, and do. If so, you'll probably only have the strength to get through the day, with little satisfaction and joy. You may fall into apathy, which literally means "unable to suffer." That is no way to live.

As much as you can, move with purpose toward your grief. If it seems unbearable to face, break it down into small doses. There is a fine line between having feelings come up and saying, "I can't deal with this right now" and denying them or saying, "I can and will deal with this for five minutes." Will yourself this strength. Act as if and face your grief. If you commit to moving in the direction of engagement, you will eventually reconcile your grief and once again feel at peace in your world.

Sometimes it helps to create a formal way to mourn. It may sound odd, but you could make a date with yourself to walk down memory lane with the person who died. Watch videos of times together, do activities you enjoyed doing together, and invite your loved one's spirit along. Ask a good friend to come over and listen to you share parts of your history. Grief can feel

Courage can't see around corners but goes around them anyway.

~ Mignon McLaughlin

When we least expect it, life sets us a challenge to test our courage and willingness to change; at such a moment, there is no point in pretending that nothing has happened or in saying that we are not yet ready. The challenge will not wait. Life does not look back.

~ Paulo Coelho

amorphous, like a huge ball of clay before it's been shaped. Molding it around an event helps you control its form, making it less intimidating and scary.

Between times of rest, also apply the idea of moving with purpose through your life. Moving with purpose means shaping your life into what you want it to be. Instead of turning on the television and watching it every evening to numb and assuage your pain and fear, do something different for at least some of that time—preferably something that is new and stimulates you. Go to the library and get lost in the shelves of books. Visit a local coffee shop and listen to music or a poetry reading. Take a hike on a nature trail. Do a hard workout at the gym. Whatever activities engage your spirit, do these as often as possible.

Personal Reflection on Courage

What is your ideal day-to-day life? What are some things you enjoyed, or were curious about, when you younger? What excites or interests you? List a few ways you can entertain these ideas, this week.

_____

_____

_____

_____

_____

_____

_____

_____

_____

_____

_____

Day 29

Bet on Yourself

Life is either a daring adventure or nothing. To keep our faces toward change and behave like free spirits in the presence of fate is strength undefeatable.

~ Helen Keller

If the person who died could give you a message from beyond, it would be this: LIVE. Live fully, deeply, daringly—as if tomorrow is your last day on earth. Do what matters. Take risks. Love, laugh, rejoice. Be your best self.

You have so much to offer in this life. While your grief may have beat you down and made you feel raw at times, it has also, paradoxically, made you stronger. As you deeply grieved and mourned, you were pushed to what you thought were your limits, yet you moved beyond them. You found out that you can handle much more than you ever imagined. You've gained wisdom and insight into what gives life meaning and what it means to live a full life.

Take these new inner strengths, insights, and beliefs and apply them to every opportunity that presents itself and every admirable desire that wishes to be filled. You have gifts and hidden talents: Discover them and put them to use. When you do so, you are committing to living your best life. This is what your soul wants, what God wants, and what the spirit of the person who died wants for you too.

Your soul has been transformed by the death of someone you love. Your soul is everything about you that is not physical— your identity, your memories, your qualities, your dreams, your values, even your sense of humor. Your soul has been transformed by suffering and surrender. When someone dies,

Our deepest fear is not that we are inadequate. Our deepest fear is that we are powerful beyond measure. It is our light, not our darkness, that frightens us. We ask ourselves 'who am I to be brilliant, gorgeous, talented and fabulous?' Actually, who are you not to be? You are a child of God. Your playing small doesn't serve the world. There's nothing enlightened about shrinking so that other people won't feel insecure around you. We were born to make manifest the glory of God that is within us... As we are liberated from our own fear, our presence automatically liberates others.

~ Marianne Williamson

we surrender to this loss, to the hole it has left in our lives. There is nothing else we can do. We learn about ourselves, life, and love through this surrender. Along the way, I hope you have surrendered self-judgment, critical thoughts, and unanswerable questions. It's time to wash yourself clean and move forward.

Through your grief journey, you have walked smack through the middle of your pain, and have come out whole, transformed, and changed. You still miss the person who died, but you have discovered courage to not only go on, but to live purposefully—courage you maybe didn't know you had. Use this courage. Bet on yourself and who you are. Remember why the person who died loved you and believed in you and be that person times ten. Move forward with gratitude for yourself and the time you were given with the person you love, and make every day count.

Personal Reflection on Courage

How has my grief transformed me and made me stronger?

_____

_____

_____

_____

_____

_____

_____

_____

_____

_____

_____

_____

Day 30

March Into the Future

Man cannot discover new oceans unless he has the courage to lose sight of the shore.

~ André Gide

Someone you love has died, and your time on earth with her has ended. This is painful and hard to accept. You have no choice but to continue on, so I encourage you to continue on as an engaged, alive human being. If you have taken the time and given the attention that's required to reconcile your hurt, pain, and grief, then you are ready to march into your new future.

You have been transformed by your grief. Your long nights of suffering have given way to a breaking dawn. Through the past days, weeks, months, or years of engaging your grief and mourning, you have integrated your loss into your life. It is still there, but it no longer overpowers you. You feel new hope and a renewed urge to welcome life and take on the joy of living.

If you are reading this and your heart is filled only with hurt and pain, you need more time to grieve and mourn. Turn back the pages and retreat into your pain. Let yourself outwardly mourn your loss. You will know when you are ready to welcome the future.

As you move forward in your grief journey, take time each day to envision your heart opening. Imagine your heart having large, double doors, and see them swinging open and releasing a bright, warm light. Now, see this light flowing out and surrounding you as you move through your day and as you connect with others, your surroundings, and nature. Feel the warm light of others and life around you flow back into your

I have accepted fear as part of life—specifically the fear of change... I have gone ahead despite the pounding in the heart that says: turn back.

~ Erica Jong

heart, making it grow brighter. Declare your daily intent to stay open and move forward by placing your hand on your heart and saying out loud: "I will let this loss open me rather than close me. I will engage in life rather than retreat from it. I will let my inner strength, courage, and resolve carry me forward."

Listen to the wisdom of your inner voice. Make choices that are congruent with what you have learned on your journey. Embrace your transformation and you will move toward greater clarity, understanding, and purpose. You will discover the future you desire. Choose life!

Personal Reflection on Courage

What are my hopes for the future? How can I welcome and engage opportunities to live fully and joyfully?

_____

_____

_____

_____

_____

_____

_____

_____

_____

_____

_____

_____

_____

_____

Closing Thoughts

Embrace an Attitude of Courage
as You Continue Your Journey

Courage is finding the inner strength and bravery required when confronting danger, difficulty, or opposition. Courage is the energy current behind all great actions and the spark that ignites the initial baby steps of growth. It resides deep within each of us, ready to be accessed in those moments when you need to forge ahead or break through seemingly insurmountable barriers. It is the intangible force that propels you forward on your journey.

~ Cherie Carter-Scott

Thank you very much for exploring this book on courage that is intended to help you on the path to relighting your divine spark. My hope is that my words have, in some small way, inspired you to not only survive, but to thrive.

Without doubt, one of my favorite definitions of courage is "the ability to do what one believes is right despite the fact that others may strongly or persuasively disagree."

I hope this resource, directed from my heart to your heart, has given you the courage to go to that spiritual place inside yourself and transcend our mourning-avoidant society. I have attempted to encourage you to gently and lovingly befriend your grief, even in a culture where some may "strongly or persuasively disagree" with your doing so.

I have attempted to help you not be ashamed of your tears and profound feelings of sadness. I have attempted to not let others succeed in efforts to move you away from your grief. Slowly, and with "no rewards for speed," you can and will return to life and begin to live again in ways that put the stars back into your sky. In following the path of your grief that allows you to do what is right for you, anchored in your unique needs, you may need to take back the authority you gave to others and place more trust in yourself.

Please remember that each of us as human beings come into the world with an organic, reliable way of integrating losses into our lives. We can authentically and openly mourn our endings. Our feelings of grief and loss help us work through the realities of death and grief. The reality that we are able to mourn tells us we were meant to befriend our life losses and "reconcile," not "resolve" them.

If we get contaminated with our society's denial of the need to mourn, we lose our courage to survive and eventually thrive in the face of what life brings us. It is up to each of us to authentically mourn the many losses, small and large, that life demands. It is up to each of us to trust that mourning is exactly how we are transformed and move through our losses toward whatever comes next in this amazing life journey. Then and only then do we no longer feel alone and isolated but reconciled in ways that reconnect us to our fellow human beings. Journey on. Godspeed.

Determination, energy, and courage appear spontaneously when we care deeply about something. We take risks that are unimaginable in any other context.

~ Margaret J. Wheatley

Personal Reflection on Courage

How can I commit myself to mustering courage as my grief
journey continues to unfold?

_____

_____

_____

_____

_____

_____

_____

_____

_____

_____

_____

_____

Start a Courage-Filled Support Group!

This book makes an ideal 12-week grief support group text. Have a get-started session, then meet once a week for 10 weeks and discuss three of the reflections each meeting. Hold a final meeting based on the Closing Thoughts section.

The Mourner's Book of Hope
30 Days of Inspiration

To integrate loss and to move forward with a life of meaning and love, you must have hope. Hope is a belief in a good that is yet to be. This beautiful little hardcover gift book offers Dr. Wolfelt's thoughts on hope in grief interspersed with quotes from the world's greatest hope-filled thinkers.

Hope begins in the dark, the stubborn hope that if you just show up and try to do the right thing, the dawn will come. You wait and watch and work: you don't give up. - Anne Lamott

Sitting in the quietness of hope encourages me to discover so many reasons to live fully until I die. - Alan D. Wolfelt

When we become aware that we do not have to escape our pains, but that we can mobilize them into a common search for life, those very pains are transformed from expressions of despair into signs of hope. - Henri Nouwen

ISBN 978-1-879651-65-4 • 200 pages • hardcover • $15.95

Companion
PRESS

All Dr. Wolfelt's publications can be ordered by mail from:
Companion Press
3735 Broken Bow Road • Fort Collins, CO 80526
(970) 226-6050 • Fax 1-800-922-6051
www.centerforloss.com

Healing Your Grieving Soul

100 Spiritual Practices for Mourners

Grief is in large part a spiritual struggle, and turning to spiritual practices in the face of loss helps many people find hope and healing. Following a helpful introduction about the role of spirituality in grief, this practical guide offers tips and activities on meditation, prayer, yoga, solitude and many more. Mourners who are feeling anxious might try breathing exercises. Those experiencing fatigue might try massage. Each idea is accompanied by a "carpe diem," which is a specific activity that the reader can try right that very moment to engage with her grief on the path to healing.

ISBN 978-1-879651-57-9 • 128 pages • softcover • $11.95

Companion
P R E S S

All Dr. Wolfelt's publications can be ordered by mail from:
Companion Press
3735 Broken Bow Road • Fort Collins, CO 80526
(970) 226-6050 • Fax 1-800-922-6051
www.centerforloss.com

Understanding Your Grief

Ten Essential Touchstones for Finding Hope and Healing Your Heart

One of North America's leading grief educators, Dr. Alan Wolfelt has written many books about healing in grief. This book is his most comprehensive, covering the essential lessons that mourners have taught him in his three decades of working with the bereaved.

In compassionate, down-to-earth language, *Understanding Your Grief* describes ten touchstones—or trail markers—that are essential physical, emotional, cognitive, social, and spiritual signs for mourners to look for on their journey through grief.

The Ten Essential Touchstones:

1. Open to the presence of your loss.
2. Dispel misconceptions about grief.
3. Embrace the uniqueness of your grief.
4. Explore what you might experience.
5. Recognize you are not crazy.
6. Understand the six needs of mourning.
7. Nurture yourself.
8. Reach out for help.
9. Seek reconciliation, not resolution.
10. Appreciate your transformation.

ISBN 978-1-879651-35-7 • 176 pages • softcover • $14.95

Companion
P R E S S

All Dr. Wolfelt's publications can be ordered by mail from:
Companion Press
3735 Broken Bow Road • Fort Collins, CO 80526
(970) 226-6050 • Fax 1-800-922-6051
www.centerforloss.com

Living in the Shadow of the Ghosts of Grief
Step into the Light

Reconcile old losses and open the door to infinite joy and love

Are you depressed? Anxious? Angry? Do you have trouble with trust and intimacy? Do you feel a lack of meaning and purpose in your life? You may well be Living in the Shadow of the Ghosts of Grief.

When you suffer a loss of any kind—whether through abuse, divorce, job loss, the death of someone loved or other transitions—you naturally grieve inside. To heal your grief, you must express it. That is, you must mourn your grief. If you don't, you will carry your grief into your future, and it will undermine your happiness for the rest of your life.

This compassionate guide will help you learn to identify and mourn your carried grief so you can go on to live the joyful, whole life you deserve.

ISBN 978-1-879651-51-7 • 160 pages • softcover • $13.95

Companion
P R E S S

All Dr. Wolfelt's publications can be ordered by mail from:
Companion Press
3735 Broken Bow Road • Fort Collins, CO 80526
(970) 226-6050 • Fax 1-800-922-6051
www.centerforloss.com

To contact Dr. Wolfelt about speaking engagements or training opportunities at his Center for Loss and Life Transition, email him at DrWolfelt@centerforloss.com.

Sayville Library
88 Greene Avenue
Sayville, NY 11782